MUSLIM FAITH
and
PRACTICE

by
MOHD. SIRAJUDDIN,
I. P. (Rtd.)

KITAB BHAVAN
NEW DELHI-110002

1982

Published by

Nusrat Ali Nasri for Kitab Bhavan
1214, Kalan Mahal, Darya Ganj, New Delhi-110002.

Printed in India

at 1711, Lahoti Fine Art Press, Suiwalan, Delhi-1100(

BISMILLAH

CONTENTS

PREFACE

To Third Edition (enlarged)

This is not a summary of a great volume of Muslim theology and practice, but a humble effort for a limited purpose. In the prevailing conditions in many non-Arab countries there are very few facilities for learning Arabic which is the language of the Muslim formal prayer. To the young people (Muslims), religious instruction at home is not also adequately available. There are different regional languages in different countries. English, however, is the most prevalent language in the world. For that reason this little volume is brought out for the benefit of those (men and women, boys and girls) who have a fair knowledge of English A Telugu version has also been brought out for the benefit of those living in my state in India (Andhra Pradesh) where the main language is Telugu. By the grace of God both versions have found general acceptance and copies of the English version are now in circulation in several countries. Many have started doing the Namaz (prayer).

I am not aware of any other handy little volume, in English or in any regional language, which describes the five important aspects of Islam in a brief and clear manner.

I wish to make clear to my readers that what I have written in Chapters I and II has the full authority of the Quran. Namaz, as I have described in Chapter III, is according to the practice of the Prophet under divine guidance and of his companions. Chapters IV and V are strictly according to history. And finally Chapter VI is entirely based on the teachings of the Quran.

In the Chapter on Namaz I have omitted some non-essential recitations to make this most holy duty clear and simple. Nothing important has been left out.

This humble work is dedicated to the service of God and His Prophet.

In the end, I am deeply grateful to my esteemed friends, Mr. V. Abdulla and Mr. Syed Ishaque for their great trouble in seeing the whole work through the press.

MOHD. SIRAJUDDIN

126 Masab Tank Road,
Hyderabad-28 (India).

19th March, 1981

CHAPTER I

It is a great blessing to be a Muslim.

Who is a Muslim?

The following are the articles of faith of a Muslim. They are simple and involve no mystery.

1 ALLAH (GOD)

Allah (God) is one, there is none to be worshipped but Allah and Muhammad is His Prophet. This is the first and the most important article of a Muslim's faith. It is called the Kalima which in Arabic reads "La ilaha Illallah Muhammadur-Rasoolullahe." God is the Lord of the universe, the ocean of mercy. It is only to Him we pray. He is not born to anyone, nor has He begotten anyone. To believe in any such relationship with reference to Him is the greatest offence to God's majesty. He is the Absolute. He does not share His sovereignty with any one, so that praying to anyone other than God is strictly forbidden, be he a demigod, prophet, saint or to anything else. I repeat; to Him only, the One God, we worship; from Him alone we seek help. This is the fundamental and basic truth of the first part of the Kalima. This article of faith is affirmed every day by a Muslim in his prayer.

2 PROPHETS

In the second part of the Kalima is the assertion that Muhammad is the Prophet of Allah. A Muslim has to believe not only in Muhammad's prophethood but also of many others, some of whose names are mentioned in the Quran—Ibrahim (Abraham), Moosa (Moses), Yahya (John), Isa

(Jesus) and others. According to the Quran, to every people and in every age, has God sent Prophets to guide them to His true religion, namely, belief in One God, to Him alone is worship due, and that this belief and worship is to be followed by righteous conduct. This was the religion taught by every one of those Prophets. But as time went on, those teachings were corrupted and the worship of one Sovereign God was substituted by worship of a host of demigods, of the so-called God's incarnations, of idols, of natural bodies like the sun, the moon, fire and of even low living creatures. It was the mission of Muhammad to lead mankind, under God's guidance, to the worship of the One True God.

3 REVELATION — (Books)

Prophets are not gods, nor are they God's incarnations. They are all human beings like Prophet Muhammad, some of whom were blessed with the gift of Revelation (Wahi, in Arabic). Thus the Revelation to Moosa is called Taurat (Torah), to Dawood Zuboor (Psalms) and to Jesus Injil (loosely called the Gospel). And finally to Muhammad was revealed the Quran. The original texts of the first three revelations no longer exist, though fragments of their teachings are scattered in the Bible and the Gospel. That is because the Christian and the Jewish scriptures have undergone several changes at human hands to suit different beliefs and doctrines at different times. But the Quran till this day, that is, from the time of its revelation 1400 years ago, remains the true record of the Divine Revelation to Muhammad, without even a word being changed. Maurice Bucaille of France, the greatest theologian of this century and an eminent doctor and scientist, records in his book *The Bible, The Quran and Science* published in U.S.A. in 1978, that in all the monotheistic religions, Quran is the only true record of the Divine Revelation. It is the last and final book revealed by

God to man, and gives complete guidance in human life in both spiritual and temporal matters.

That Quran is the true and final word of God is an article of Muslim faith.

4 ANGELS

They are the spiritual agencies of God for communicating with human beings. They had brought God's message to Prophets as was the case with Angel Jibrail (Gabriel) who had brought the Quranic Revelation to Muhammad. They had brought messages to Abraham and Lut, Mary and others too. Angels are not God's partners, nor are they objects of worship.

5 THE DAY OF JUDGEMENT

On the belief in Judgement Day rests the whole structure of a Muslim's life and conduct. There is life after death for human beings, when they are called on to account for their actions during their life on earth.

Good life is according to the Quran, rewarded with spiritual felicity and peace and evil one punished.

On Judgement Day, it is the rule of accountability that prevails, which means that each individual has to answer for his or her actions on earth. There is thus no vicarious atonement nor intercession in Islam. In other words, one person's suffering or even death, or his charities do not lead to the salvation of another; nor can one, be he a saint (living or dead), murshad pir, swami or a priest of the highest order, intercede with God for another's salvation nor can grant absolution. "Who is there that can intercede in His Presence except as He permitteth" says the Quran (II/255) — which means forgiveness is with God alone. Man attains grace solely by his own moral endeavour. God is the All-Merciful, and it is to Him alone should man pray for forgiveness, and for His bounty. "Call upon Me, I will answer your prayer"—says God in the Quran.

Says He further: "I am nearer to you than your jugular vein — I listen to the prayer of every suppliant that calleth on Me — Remember Me; I will remember you. . . .

Need human beings then ever be in despair or feel helpless in life's stresses! God's mercy is boundless and is on those that turn to Him.

It should be noted that life after death does not mean rebirth on this earth in any form.

The religion followed by Muslims is called Islam, a name given to it by God. Islam means obedience or submission, and also means peace which follows obedience to God's commandments and the Prophet's teachings. It is this religion that every Prophet had preached before Muhammad, but had become corrupt and idolatrous during succeeding centuries.

CHAPTER II

The Pillars of Islam

To lead a good life, mere beliefs are not sufficient. Four very important obligatory religious duties towards God are also prescribed.

They are: —

1 PRAYER: called Salat in Arabic and Namaz in Persian. As namaz is a widely understood term, I shall be using that term in this book.

Though namaz is the most important of the obligatory duties, for the sake of convenience I shall describe it in Chapter III.

2 FAST: Saum in Arabic. The Urdu speaking people call it Roza. Muslims have to observe fast for the whole month of Ramzan. This month is sacred because the first verses of the Quran were revealed to the Prophet in this month. During the fast nothing should be taken by way of food or drink from one and a half hours before sunrise until after sunset. Even smoking is not permitted. All the five prayers for the day should be performed. It should be a clean day-to-day life without lying, cheating, violence and other evil acts. Only those who are ill or on a journey and also women during their monthly course, are exempted from fasting but they should make up the lost days by fasting on other days. Before breaking the fast with a little clean food or drink, a prayer to God that the fast may be accepted, is recommended. This is also the moment for your personal supplications to God. After breaking the fast, Maghrib namaz

(sunset prayers) should be done. Later at any time regular food may be taken. Before commencement of the fast you are permitted to have a meal. To those who fast, it is a period of great spiritual uplift.

The institution of fasting during Ramzan is not for penitence (expiation) or penance, and certainly not for corporal mortification. In Islam fasting is an act of abstinence that we may practice piety by restraining our senses and appetites for a fixed number of days.

On the day following the month-long fast is the festival (Eid-ul-fitr) commonly known as Ramzan Eid. The Eid prayer is described at the end of the chapter on namaz.

3 ZAKAAT: Prior to Islam no religion had made succour to the widow, the orphan and the helpless — the highest form of charity — an obligatory duty.

Zakaat is broadly translated as charity. In Islam charity is not limited to mere giving of money to the needy. It very much includes human help, one to the other, in different ways — monetary, physical, material and mental. All this comes under Zakaat. The basis of our religion is service to others. It is the duty of the rich to help the poor. There is no limit to charity or Zakaat. In monetary terms, a minimum is fixed which is $2\frac{1}{2}\%$ of one's income or residual wealth. Zakaat in Islam is actually a social right on the wealth of the rich.

Zakaat is fundamentally an act of worship. Zakaat means "to purify". "Zakaat purifies our soul". This is an excellent institution for the welfare of society. The importance of Zakaat will be noticed from the fact that in the Quran, Salat and Zakaat are often mentioned together. For the first time in the history of religious development, this right of the poor on the rich and this principle of mutual help are made a Farz — meaning obligatory duty — in human conduct.

4 HAJJ

Hajj is the pilgrimage to Makka, obligatory on all Muslims, at least once in their life-time, means and health permitting. It is a religious duty. About two thousand five hundred years before the birth of Prophet Muhammad, a great Prophet called Ibrahim (Abraham) and his son Ismail built under God's command the First House of Worship of the One God, at Makka, which is in Arabia. It was a simple four walled stone structure and was called Kaaba. Gradually during succeeding centuries this House of God's Worship became the house of idol worship, and continued to be so till Muhammad's time. The Prophet however started preaching Islam from the Kaaba, and in due course cleansed it of all idols. And ever since, it has been the spiritual centre for the Muslims who from all over the world, irrespective of colour or race, meet here on equal terms in the month of Zul Hajj of the Islamic calendar, and pray to God. Thus Hajj is a great spiritual experience. This is the occasion for celebrating all over the world the Eid commonly known as Bakrid. The correct name is Eid-uz-Zuha. This Eid prayer is the same as that of Eid-ul-Fitr.

5. The above four duties along with the Kalima constitute the Five Pillars of Islam; the Kalima, Namaz, Saum, Zakaat and Hajj.

Duties towards fellow beings are described in Chapter VI.

CHAPTER III

NAMAZ, SALAT (Prayer)

My young friends, do not be discouraged at what appears to be a long chapter. I have tried to make things clear in this most important duty of a Muslim. You will feel better when you read the last paragraph of the section Supplementary Prayers of this chapter. Just get by heart the two Suras mentioned in this chapter, and also the other two or three texts; the whole prayer then becomes easy. Arabic is such a language that if you read a passage five or six times it comes by heart. I have made this chapter concise and nothing important is omitted.

A Muslim's prayer (namaz) is a direct communion between him and his Creator. He affirms God's glory and omnipotence and, at the same time, seeks humbly and earnestly His blessings, guidance, forgiveness and protection. There is no intermediary between him and God. There is therefore no priestly establishment class or caste in Islam, claiming special holiness or special spiritual privileges. Even in congregational prayers or on ceremonial occasions, any Muslim can lead the former or conduct the latter.

Women are exempted from namaz during menstrual course.

There are four postures in namaz, all signifying humility.

1. Standing: — Head covered, feet a little apart, face to the Kaaba, fore-arms one above the other on the navel. Women fold their arms on their chest. The Kaaba is to the west from India. This position is called Qiyam.

2. Bending: — Keep each palm just above the knee cap, and legs straight. This position is called Ruku.

3. Prostrating: — Knees on the ground, forehead and nose touching the ground, arms bent and palms resting on the ground on either side of the head. This is called Sajda.

4. Squatting on the ground after each sajda, buttocks resting on the feet in a convenient position, and palms on the thighs. This is called Q'ada.

Namaz is done five times a day at:

1. Fajr (Half an hour before sunrise)
2. Zuhr (Early after-noon)
3. Asr (Late after-noon)
4. Maghrib (Soon after sunset) and
5. Isha (Between one and a half hours after sunset and two and a half hours before sunrise. Normally, this prayer is done between two to four hours after sunset.

Cleanliness of body and clothing is essential before commencing namaz. If a person has had sexual intercourse or has come from a long journey, or after the menstrual course, he or she should have a complete bath after gargling, and rinsing the nostrils. Otherwise, a person with normal cleanliness should do what is called Wazoo before doing his prayers. Wazoo consists essentially of washing the forearms, face, passing wet hands over the upper portion of the head and over ears and neck, to remove dust (this is called Masah), and washing the feet. To this add rinsing the mouth and the nostrils, and wazoo is complete. It will be necessary to do wazoo again after any call of nature is answered. If socks are worn after a bath or a day's first wazoo, in a subsequent wazoo feet need not be washed again so long as socks are worn. For a Muslim "cleanliness is next to Godliness". That is why normally a Muslim invariably washes the part after passing urine.

Namaz can be done on any clean place, in a mosque, one's house or in any open space. It is divided into parts called rakaats, and each of the five prayers has two, three or four rakaats. These are described below.

Namaz is of two kinds: One obligatory (called Farz); and two supernumerary (recommended). In form and content both are similar.

Namaz of Two Rakaats

After wazoo, stand on one end of the prayer mat facing the Kaaba. Lift each of your palms to the ears, and while doing so say Allaho-Akbar (God is the greatest). Allaho-Akbar is called Takbeer. After saying the takbeer place your forearms on the navel, the right on the left. Then say the following prayer.

Subhanaka Alla Humma Wa Behamdeka Wa Tabarkasmoka Wa Ta' Ala Jaddoka Wa La Ilaha Ghairoka

(All glory and praise to You, O Allah. Blessed is Your name and exalted is Your Majesty. There is none worthy of worship except You).

The above prayer is called SANA.

After reading the SANA read the following:

Auzo Billahe Minash Shaitan Ir Rajim

(I seek refuge of Allah against Satan who has been rejected by Him).

Then read the following:

Bismillah Ir Rahman Ir Rahim

(I begin with the name of Allah, who is most beneficient and merciful). Then read the first Sura (Chapter) from the Quran given below. It is called Sura Fatiha or briefly Fatiha. This is an obligatory part of every namaz.

Sura-e-Fateha

Alhamdo Lillahi Rabbil 'Alamin. Ar Rahmanir Rahim. Malik-E-Yaumiddin Iyyaka Na' Budo Wa Iyyaka Nasta' In. Ihdinas Siratal Mustaqima Siratallazina An' Amta Alaihim Ghairil Maghdubi Alaihim Wa Laddalin. Ameen.

(All praise to God, the Cherisher and Sustainer of the worlds, Most Gracious, Most Merciful. Ruler of the Day of Judgement. O Allah, Thee alone do we worship and of Thee alone do we seek help. Guide us in the path that is right and straight, the path of those on whom Thou hast bestowed Thy grace; not of those whose portion is wrath, nor of those who have gone astray).

After reading the above, read the following Sura:

Qul Huwallaho Ahad. Allah-Hus-Samad. Lam Yalid Walam Yulad. Walam Yakun-Lahu-Kufu-Wan Ahad.

(Say, He is Allah the only One to be worshipped, Allah the Eternal and sought by all. He begets not, nor is He begotten, and there is none like Him). This is called SURA-e-IQLAS. If you know any other small Sura you may read it, instead. The above good Sura is by way of an example.

After reading the above two Suras say the takbeer (this time you need not raise your palms to your ears) and get into the posture of RUKU. In this position say thrice the following:—

Subhana Rabbi Yal Azim

(Glory to my Lord who is great).

After that stand up saying:

Sami Alla Ho Liman Hameda

(God has heard me, who has glorified Him).

Follow this by exclaiming:

Rabbana Lakal Hamd

(Our Creator and Cherisher, all praise and thankfulness are to You).

After this say the takbeer and get into the posture of Sajdah. In this position say the following thrice:

Subhana Rabbiyal 'Ala

(Glory to my Lord who is most high).

After saying the above, say the takbeer and sit for a second, again say the takbeer and do a second sajdah repeating,

Subhana Rabbiyal A'la (thrice)

After this say takbeer, stand up and assume the posture of Qiyam. This is the end of the first rakaat, and the beginning of the second in every namaz.

In namaz of two rakaats continue as follows:

Read the Fatiha and second sura and continue the namaz as in the first rakaat. After the second sajdah sit in the posture of Q'ada and read the following which is referred to as Attahiyyat.

At-Tahiyyato Lillahi Wassalawatu Wat-Taiyyibatu Assalamu Alaika Ayyu-Han-Nabiyyu Wa Rahma-

tullahi Wa Barakatuho. Assalamu Alaina Wa Ala Ibadillah-Is-Saliheen. Ash-Hadu An Laa Ilaha Ill-Allaho Wa Ash-Hadu Anna Muhammadan Abdu Hoo Wa Rasoolohu.

(All reverence, all worship, all sanctity are due to Allah. Peace be on you O Prophet and the Mercy of Allah and His blessings. Peace be on us and all the righteous servants of Allah. I bear witness that none is deserving of worship except Allah and I also bear witness that Muhammad is His servant and Prophet.)

After the above read the following which is called Darood-e-Ibrahim.

Allahumma Salli Ala Muhammadin Wo Ala Aali Muhammadin Kama Sallaita Ala Ibrahima Wa Ala Aali Ibrahima Innaka Hamidum Majeed. Allahumma Barik Ala Muhammadin Wa Ala Aali Muhammadin Kama Barakta Ala Ibrahima Wa Ala Aali Ibrahima Innaka Hamidum Majeed.

(O Allah! Shower your blessings on Muhammad and his descendants as You had showered Your blessings on Ibrahim and his descendants; verily, to You is the praise and the glory.

O Allah! bless Muhammad and his descendants as You had blessed Ibrahim and his descendants; verily, to You is the praise and the glory.)

This is followed by a small prayer:

Rabbana Aatina Fiddunya Hasantan Wa Fil Akhirate Hasanatan Waqina Azabannar.

(Our Lord, give us goodness in this world and in the world hereafter, and save us from hell.) If you know any other prayer, you may read that instead. After that turn you face to the right and then to the left each time saying:

Assalamu 'Alaikum Wa Rahmatullah.

(Peace be upon you and the mercy of Allah). This is called Salaam.

This ends a two rakaat namaz. After namaz (whether of two, three or four rakkats) you may sit for a little while and pray to Allah in your own words for whatever you wish.

Four Rakaat Namaz

Till after you read Attahiyyat in the second rakkaat, the form of prayer in the first two rakaats in this namaz is the same as in the two rakaat namaz. After reading the Attahiyyat stand up saying the takbeer and read only the Fatiha and then do the ruku and the sajdah. After the second sajdah at the end of this (third) rakaat, stand again saying the takbeer and continue the last rakaat. After the second sajdah in this final rakaat sit and read Attahiyyat, Darood Ibrahim and the prayer, and say the salaam turning your face to both sides. This completes the four rakaat namaz.

Three Rakaat Namaz

The mode of this namaz too is the same. After the second sajdah in the third rakaat sit in Q'ada, read the Attahiyyat, Darood Ibrahim and the prayer (Rabbana Astina) and complete the namaz by saying the salaam.

In addition to these obligatory (called Farz) prayers, there are supernumerary prayers which can wait until after you fully learn to do the Farz namaz. Their mode however is the same.

Namaz in a Mosque

What is described above is when you do the prayers individually in places other than the mosque. The Farz namaz in a mosque is congregational. One person who is called the Imam leads the prayers. The procedure is somewhat different but the form of the namaz is the same (This procedure is also followed when two or more persons do the Farz namaz together outside a mosque.)

The Imam stands in front, and behind him in straight consecutive rows stand the others. The Imam says the takbeer and others follow, saying the same. Now note carefully. During the morning, sunset and night prayers, the Imam after reading the SANA, AUZO BILLAH and BISMILLAH to himself, reads the Fatiha and the second sura aloud in the first two rakaats. During the remaining third and fourth rakaats he reads the Fatiha in a low tone. What you do is when he reads aloud in the first two rakaats you listen quietly and just say Ameen after the sura Fatiha. And when he reads the Fatiha quietly in the third and fourth rakaats you too read the Fatiha in a low tone. The rest is simple. After takbeer by the Imam, you say it too and follow his movements and read in the ruku, sajdah and q'ada what I have described above in the procedure for doing the namaz. And when he says the salaam you too say the salaam. At the end of the namaz the Imam says a collective prayer to God, and you say Ameen. The Farz namaz in the mosque is ended.

NOTE: If you go to a mosque twice the above procedure will come to you easily.

Juma Prayers

Of all the prayers done in a mosque, Juma prayers which are held on Fridays are important and should not normally be missed. After Azan (call to prayer) the congregation individually does four rakaats of supernumerary (Sunnat) namaz. The form and content of these prayers are the same as in the Farz prayers. After this Sunnat namaz, the Imam delivers a sermon (called Quthba). Then he leads two rakaats of Farz prayers, after which you may do four plus two rakaats of Sunnat namaz. With this the Juma prayers which normally take about forty minutes are over.

Here I may add that in Juma prayers, Farz are only two, namely listening to the Quthba, and doing two rakaat namaz following the Quthba. The rest are recommended supernumerary prayers. Juma prayer replaces the day's Zuhr namaz.

My young friends and others, I request you earnestly to start on Farz prayers which do not take long. The two rakaat prayer takes only three minutes and four rakaat only five minutes. For earning God's blessings, and expressing our humility and gratitude, the time spent in prayer, which is our foremost duty, is very little.

If any namaz except Juma namaz is unavoidably missed, it may be done at the next prayer time.

Supernumerary Prayers

They are called Sunnat, Nafil and Wajib. Whether you do these additional prayers or not, Farz namaz is obligatory. As I have said earlier, there is no difference between the supernumerary and Farz namaz. The number of rakaats and their sequence at the different prayer times are as follows:

Fajr	... 2 Sunnat and 2 Farz
Zuhr	... 4 Sunnat 4 Farz and 2 Sunnat
Asr	... 4 Farz

Maghrib ... 3 Farz and 2 Sunnat
Isha ... 4 Farz 2 Sunnat and 3 Wajib

In the above I have omitted 2 rakaats of Nafil prayers which are purely voluntary and which are said at the end of Maghrib, Isha and Juma prayers.

Wajib namaz which is highly recommended, is done on three occasions — on the two Eid days and during Isha prayer. The latter is a three rakaat namaz said after the two rakaat Sunnat prayer. In the third rakaat after sura Fatiha and a second sura say the takbeer and raise your palms to your ears, then fold your arms again on the navel and read a prayer called Qunnooth which I give below. After you read it, say the takbeer, go into ruku and finish the prayer. (IF YOU DO NOT KNOW OR REMEMBER THIS QUNNOOTH PRAYER, READ THE PRAYER RABBANA AATINA — which is given earlier while describing two rakaat namaz).

Dua-e-Qunnooth

Alla Humma-Inna Nastayeenoka Va-Nastaghfiroka, Vanumenu Bika Va-Natavakkalo-Alaika, Vanusni Alaikal Qair-Vanash-Kuruka Valaa Nakfuruka-Vanaqlavo-Vanathroka My-Yaf Joroka-Alla Humma, Iyyaka Nabudo-Valaka Nusalli-Va Nasjudo Va Ilaika, Nusaa-Va Nah Fido-Va Narju-Rah-Mataka-Va Nakqsha Azabaka, Inna Azabaka-Bil Kuffare Mulhiq.

(O Allah, we seek Thy aid and Thy forgiveness. We believe in Thee, praise Thee and are grateful to Thee. Keep us away from those who disobey THEE.

We worship only Thee, we fear and obey Thee, and strive to obtain Thy grace. Thy punishment is for the unbelievers.)

During the month of **Ramzan**, if you fast and go to the mosque for Isha namaz, there is a congregational prayer of twenty rakaats done after the two Sunnat rakaats. This is called Namaz-e-Taravih. You will get to know this later. Also, the Wajib namaz is done with the Imam only during Ramzan month in the mosque. At all other times it is done individually.

This is the end of supernumerary prayers. Once again I wish to impress on you that if you miss these supernumerary prayers due to want of time or any other reason, you are not guilty of any serious lapse. What is important is, you should not miss the Farz namaz. Some of these supernumerary prayers were performed by the Prophet.

Namaz-e-Eid-ul-Fitr, and **Eid-uz-Zuha** (called Bakrid)

Eid namaz is not Farz (obligatory) but is highly recommended (Wajib). It is performed in open maidans to permit large gatherings, and also in mosques. The two occasions are Eid-ul-Fitr and Bakrid during a year. This namaz is similar to the every-day namaz and is described below.

Each of the two Eid prayers has two rakaats which are conducted by an Imam, in the same manner as is done in a regular two rakaat namaz in a mosque. There is however one difference. In each of the two rakaats three additional takbeers (Allah-o-Akbar) are said, as described below.

In the first rakaat, after the SANA is read following the initial takbeer, the Imam says Allah-o-Akbar loudly, lifts his hands to his ears and drops them to his sides. You too do the same after saying the takbeer. The imam does this a second time and you follow him. For the third time he says the takbeer, but after that he places his fore-arms on his navel. You do the same. After this the first rakaat is gone through in the usual manner.

In the second rakaat, only after the Fatiha and the second sura are read by the Imam, are the additional three takbeers said. The imam says the first takbeer and keeps standing with hands down; you too do the same. This is repeated twice. On the fourth takbeer the entire congregation go into ruku, and complete the rakaat.

After this, the assembly keep sitting while the Imam delivers a sermon (Qutba) on the significance and importance of the occasion, followed by a prayer. This ends the Eid namaz. You then meet as many of those assembled as you can, and wish them Eid Mubarak.

In India women generally do not join the men-folk in Eid namaz. They do the namaz individually in their houses, while the men are doing theirs. In U.K., U.S.A. and other places women join in this namaz.

Namaz-e-Janaza

(Prayer for the dead)
Janaza means coffin

This is a prayer for God's mercy on the soul or souls of the dead, usually said in the open front space of a mosque with the coffin also placed there in the view of those who pray.

This namaz is congregational in which the Imam leads, the rest standing behind him in straight rows. The entire namaz is done in standing position with arms folded on the navel, and has in it four takbeers. The prayer is simple.

After the first takbeer by the Imam and the rest, the SANA is read softly by all. At the other three takbeers, hands are not raised to the ears, as at the first takbeer, but only the face is lifted a little for a second.

You have already learnt the SANA in the chapter on NAMAZ. You have learnt Darood-e-Ibrahim too.

After the SANA is read, the Imam and the rest say the second takbeer, after which Darood-e-Ibrahim is **read in** soft tones by every one.

Then follows the third takbeer and the following prayer is said by every one in a soft tone:

Allahummaghfir Lehayyena Wa Mayyetena Wa Shahedena Wa Ghaibena Wa Saghirena Wa Kabirena Wa Zakerena Wa Unsana. Allahumma Man Ahyaitahu Minna Faahyihi Alalislame Wa Man Tawoffaitahu Minna Fatamaffohu Alaliman.

I give below the substance of the above prayer.

"O Allah forgive the deceased. Forgive our living and the dead, men and women, young and old, male and female, and those present and those that are absent. Merciful God, grant us life and death in Islam."

If you do not remember this prayer in Arabic, then say its substance with the utmost sincerity in any language you know best.

After the above prayer follows the final takbeer. A second later the Imam and the rest say the salaam turning their faces to either side.

Assalamu Alaikum Wa Rahmatullah

(God's mercy and peace be on you)

This ends namaz-e-Janaza. You may then follow the coffin to the graveyard which is generally closeby, and join in the burial ceremony.

This namaz is not a Farz (obligatory) prayer, but is an important one for a Muslim. To every one of us comes this end. It is therefore good to keep in mind that we too after death need the earnest prayers of the living. When you see a coffin being carried, say the salaam to the one inside it, and if possible help in carrying it to a short distance. Also when you pass a graveyard, do not fail to say the salaam to the denizens of the graves.

Gentle reader, God's blessings be on you in this world and in the next. He is the Ocean of Mercy.

CHAPTER IV

A Brief Account of the Prophet's Life

When one writes on Prophet Muhammad's life and teachings, one is on firm ground of history — not on mystery and miracle, fable and folklore clouding the reality, as has been the case with the earlier Prophets and religious teachers.

Prophet Muhammad (peace be on him) was born in the year 570 A.D. at Makka in the family of the Quraish which was highly respected throughout Arabia as they were the custodians of the Kaaba. You have read briefly about the Kaaba in Chapter II under Hajj. As his father died before his birth and his mother six years later, he came under his grandfather's guardianship. When the latter died two years later, his uncle Abu Talib became his guardian.

His early years were uneventful which were spent away from Makka in the care of his foster-mother, as was the custom then in respectable Makkan families. From his young age he was closely associated with his uncle whom he accompanied on business trips to Syria and other places, which helped to broaden his mind and understanding. He was always very correct and honest in his dealings, ever helpful to others, young and old, and extremely trustworthy so that he came to be known early as Al Amin, The Trustworthy. Impressed by his excellent character and behaviour, Khadija, a well-to-do widow of a noble family, invited him to marry her, which he did. He was then twenty-five and Khadija some years older. It was a happy marriage. She bore him four daughters, and one son Khasim who died in infancy. The well known Fatima was their youngest daughter. He was a devoted husband and a loving father. Though he had other wives after Khadija's death, only one, Maria, bore him a son Ibrahim who too died in infancy. His youngest wife was Aisha, an accomplished lady, the daughter of Abu Bakar who later became the first Khalif.

Geographically, Arabia was an isolated country, the only contacts with the outside world being occasional trade caravans. Like many countries far and near, especially the whole of Europe which was then in its Dark Ages, Arabia was a backward country. Though the Arabs had some fine virtues of bravery, sportsmanship, hospitality, love for poetry etc., they had several evil ways. They were idol worshippers too. Kaaba which was the first House of Worship of The One God, became through the centuries the house of hundreds of idols which the Arabs worshipped. Muhammad however kept aloof from idol worship from his boyhood. He became increasingly contemplative and alive to the existence of One Supreme Being to whom alone worship was due. He frequently visited the cave in Mount Hira which was about three miles from Makka, and spent nights and days there in meditation. His life throughout was one of highest rectitude. At the age of forty when he was meditating in the cave of Hira, he received one night the first Revelation. That was during the last week of the month of Ramzan. Muhammad was much frightened at this extraordinary experience but his noble wife Khadija gave him comfort and courage, and assured him that he was the Prophet of God. From that day Muhammad entered on his mission of Prophethood. God was one, and none was to be worshipped but God.

From the beginning his task was difficult. All Makkans turned against him. Firstly, they were not prepared to give up idol worship, which was their ancient custom. Secondly, if they did give it up, the importance of Kaaba which contained three hundred and sixty-five idols which the Arabs worshipped would diminish in the eyes of the Arabs, and their annual pilgrimage would cease resulting in severe economic loss to Makka. Muhammad and his small but slowly growing number of followers in faith, were subjected to increasing harassment and cruelty. They had to do the worship of God in secrecy. There was however a respite when the redoubtable Umar, hitherto a bitter opponent, accepted the faith. Even this respite was short-lived. Unable to live under these hard conditions, a big group of Muslims, men and women, migrated to Abyssinia where they were treated kindly by the Christian ruler Negus. In Makka severe persecution and cruelty continued. From the time of the first revelation, it was thirteen long and cruel years for the Prophet and many of his followers. He therefore decided to migrate to Madina, a town about three hundred and seventy-five miles to the north, permitting such of his followers as wished to, also to migrate. Some of the important citizens of Madina who had come to believe in the Prophet during their earlier pilgrimages to Makka, had invited him to Madina where they promised all help. At considerable personal risk Muhammad left Makka with his close friend Abu Bakar and reached Madina. Some of the faithful had preceded him and several others followed. These early emigrants were called Muhajirs, meaning those who migrated. The Madinites were as good as their word and gave them all help. From that day they were called Ansar, meaning helpers. This emigration in 622 A.D., called Hijrath, was the turning point in the history of Islam. This was also the beginning of the Hijra calendar of the Muslims. From that time onwards for ten years, that is, for the remainder of the Prophet's life, it was the period for the flowering of Islam, and the fulfilment of the Prophet's mission.

Muhammad organised the living conditions of the newly arrived Muslims with the whole-hearted help of the Ansar. The number of those who joined the faith was rising rapidly. The Makkans however would not leave Muhammad and his followers in peace. At the end of the first year of the Hijra, the Makkan army, a thousand strong, marched on Madina to destroy this small community of Muslims. The Prophet could muster only 313, old and young, to face the enemy on the plain of Badr about 80 miles from Madina. This was the first and the most crucial battle in the history of Islam, because on its result depended the survival or the end of the faith. The enemy's fairly well equipped forces were thrice the size of the Muslims whose equipment and strength were only their courage, and faith in God and His Prophet. That courage and faith prevailed and the enemy were routed with their leader dead on the battlefield. This was the famous battle of Badr which changed the history of the world for the better.

Incensed at their defeat, the Makkans came again the following year with an army of three thousand, and met the Muslim forces which started a thousand strong but was depleted by treachery to about seven hundred. This was on the plain near Mount Uhad, two miles from Madina. Both sides suffered serious casualties, the Prophet was wounded, and the result was indecisive. Though the advantage was with the enemy, for some inexplicable reason, they withdrew in the night and returned to Makka. During the succeeding years there were several other battles big and small, all generally ending in success for the Muslims. It should be noted that the battles were mostly in self-defence or for violation of treaties. The Jews who were inimical to the Muslims from the early Madina days as they had lost all their influence in the area with the arrival of the Prophet, were a constant source of trouble and treachery. In the 8th year AH consequent to the violation of treaty pledges by the Makkans, the Prophet marched against Makka, his cruel home city which he had to leave as a fugitive, and occupied it. The manner in which this enemy city was occupied has no parallel in world's history.

There was clemency for everyone and a general amnesty was proclaimed. Not a life was lost. None was molested. Impressed by the Prophet's great forbearance, all the Makkans embraced Islam. Kaaba was cleansed of all idols and Muhammad led the prayers there at the head of a very large congregation. After halting for some days and leaving Makka in charge of a governor, the Prophet returned to Madina to the great delight of the Ansar, thus allaying their fears that he would stay on in his home city.

In 631 A.D. a year before his death, the Prophet again went to Makka, this time on pilgrimage which is known as the Farewell Hajj. During the world famous sermon which he delivered to a gathering of about 1,25,000 at the time of this Hajj, he stressed on the equality of man, and on the social duties of the Islamic brotherhood which by then had comprised most of Arabia, and which in the years to come was to become a World Brotherhood. After his return to Madina he died in the year 632 A.D. and was buried in his wife Aisha's room where he had taken ill and breathed his last. He was 63 according to the Islamic calendar. His mission on earth was completed. Of no other Prophet has there been such a truly historical account, free from fable, mystery and miracle, as of Mohammad's life and mission.

The ten years of his life at Madina were of unparalleled activity on his part. His fame had spread and an ever-increasing number of Arabs accepted the new faith on account of its catholicity and just practices. The Prophet became both the spiritual and temporal head. A small mosque of thatch and mud was first built after his arrival there, which soon became the nerve centre of the new faith and where he later conducted political and economic affairs, receiving envoys and planning campaigns. This small structure has grown through the centuries into the world-famous Prophet's Mosque of today called Masjid-e-Nabvi. Madina soon grew into a city, and its civic and social needs had to be attended to. A written constitution was drawn up by the Prophet for this small city-state, defining the rights and duties of the majority and the minorities, the latter comprising mostly of Jews and Christians, guaranteeing their safety, property and religion. This written constitution, the first of its kind in the world, is preserved to this day in the original Arabic. Rights of minorities and of vanquished people were unknown prior to Islam, and it was this that drew many into its fold. Rapidly the religion spread, with all the Arab tribes accepting it, and by the time of the Prophet's death, ten years after his arrival in Madina, the whole of Arabia accepted the faith. Muhammad thus became the undisputed ruler of this large country. No other Prophet before him had seen such a magnificent completion of his mission during his lifetime.

Islam's Achievement

Within a period of ten years idol worship was eliminated from the entire Arabian Peninsula, and during the succeeding years a quarter of the world's population would prostrate before the One and only God — Absolute and Supreme. Human mind was finally liberated from the trammels of fetish fiction and multiplicity of gods and goddesses. Human dignity was once again restored. Woman was raised from the age-long status of a chattel to that of legal equality with man, something unknown before the advent of Islam and for many centuries subsequent to it. Acquisition of knowledge was given very high priority, even if it involved trouble and distant travel. As a result of all this, the hitherto illiterate Arabs became thirsty for knowledge and they in turn brought knowledge and light to the Dark Ages of Europe. And the greatest achievement of all was, for the first time in history, Islam knit the human race into one brotherhood. There was no more distinction of race, colour or status. The result was the coming into existence of a world-society in which prince and peasant prostrated side by side in prayer, and in which slaves were nominated as kings and queens and as commanders of large armies — a phenomenon unknown in non-Muslim world. For this unprecedented achievement, the foundation was the teaching of the Quran and the Prophet.

CHAPTER V

The Quran

The Quran is like no other scripture. It is not like the Jewish Scripture which is a semi-historical and legendary narrative beginning from the world's "creation" to the time of the arrival of the Jews in the Promised Land (roughly, modern Israel) after their release from Egyptian captivity, and also an account of their Prophets and Kings, their laws, their travails and their triumphs, and also their moral lapses — all written by different persons over a period of several centuries. Nor is it like the New Testament which comprises chiefly of the four gospels which give a brief history of Jesus, especially of his short ministry and his teachings, which were chronicled by different individuals very long after his death, and which differ in important particulars. Nor is it like the Hindu Vedas and Upanishads which contain accounts and descriptions of the earliest forms of worship, rituals, different kinds of philosophical and scientific thought, and also two great epic poems — all written and added to during successive centuries. Nor like the Buddhist scripture too. This came first to be written several hundred years after Buddha's death, so that fact, tradition and folklore all combined in the writing of that scripture, which during the succeeding centuries was further added to by various individuals, as the original faith itself gradually divided itself into two schools of thought. The Quran, on the other hand, is a word-for-word record made then and there of the revelations received by the Prophet during the twenty-three years of his ministry, not a word of which has been altered during the past 1400 years. The revelations came as occasion demanded, as the Muslim community and religion developed from infancy to maturity.

Muhammad is not the author of the Quran. It is God who is its author. That it is the word of God is affirmed in several places in the Quran. Muhammad himself hardly knew how to read and write. It is relevant to mention here what Maurice Bucaille, the great theologian referred to in Chapter I under Revelation, has to say. In Divine Revelation there can be neither inaccuracy nor inconsistency. Both these however abound in other scriptures. This has been specially so in matters relating to scientific facts. The *several* and varied statements made in those scriptures relating to physical sciences and other events are all scientifically incorrect. Whereas, in the Quran there are *innumerable* references to physical and natural sciences all of which are correct by the present day scientific criteria. And what is more, these statements were made at a time (early in the 7th century A.D.) when human knowledge was very limited throughout the world, particularly so in the large desert country of Arabia where the Quranic Revelation came. And so Bucaille draws the irresistible conclusion that what was established as scientific facts by the highly developed modern sciences, can only be super-human knowledge at the time it was revealed 1400 years ago. Thus he concludes, in all monotheistic religions Quran is the only true record of Divine Revelation. There can be no other conclusion. Its tone and style throughout are so sublime and so unique that even the greatest Arabic scholars have not been able to achieve a fraction of this sublimity during all the centuries. It is therefore referred to as the Glorious Quran. Says God in the Quran (17/88), "Not all the mankind and Jinns together can produce the like of the Quran". It's sublime character apart, as a complete code of spiritual, moral, ethical and social guidance for all humanity, it has no equal. And its clarity and lucidity are superb.

During the life-time of the Prophet, the entire Quran was preserved in writing as well as in the memory of a large number of his close associates and followers. After Muhammad's death, during the early campaigns at the time of Khalif Abu Bakar, several of the Hafizes died. (A Hafiz is one who has memorised the whole Quran.) The sagacious Umar, who was to be the next Khalif, then prevailed upon Abu Bakar to have the Quranic records collected and compiled into a book form. This was done. The best and well known Hafizes assisted in this great work. Towards the close of his life, the Prophet himself had indicated the sequence of the Quranic chapters and their verses. Not a single verse was omitted. Later during the time of the third Khalif Usman, many more identical copies were made as there was a great demand for them from the conquered countries. One of these copies is today in the Istambul museum in Turkey. It is nearly 1400 years now, but not a word has changed despite billions of copies being published throughout the world during these centuries. It is God's promise in the Quran (15/9) that He will preserve the integrity of the Quran through the ages.

Yousuf Ali's English translation of the Quran is very lucid and informative and can be read with profit. Maulana Mohd. Ali's translation is also good. While studying either, careful attention should be paid to foot-notes and explanations of incidents referred to in the Quran. The translations by Europeans, except those by Arberry and one or two others, have a basic overtone of bias, hostility and wrong presentation.

CHAPTER VI

The Ethics of Islam

It was during the decades and centuries that followed the original dispensation of all religions, that the great bulk of the religious, moral and social precepts as we have them today, have been added to or written by different persons — EXCEPT in the case of Islam, where right at the beginning a complete code of human conduct in all spheres was revealed. Amongst all the religions of the world, only in Islam was the greatest emphasis laid on duties towards, and service to, fellow human beings, right at the beginning of this unique dispensation. There is thus no other original scripture comparable to Quran. There are also the Prophet's teachings based on the Quran. Both these are the solid base of Muslim ethics.

In Islam mere abstract belief has no moral value or meaning, if it is not followed by right conduct. There is no compromise on this. What is right conduct is clearly stated in the pages of the Quran. I give below a few of its precepts.

a) Love and respect for parents, and their care at all times. This is emphasised repeatedly in the Quran, and is the first injunction in the Muslim code of conduct. When asked about Paradise, the Prophet said "Paradise is under the feet of the mother". This saying applies equally to one's father too. The Quran repeatedly lays emphasis on reverence and care for parents. And in Sura 31/14 God particularly says "Show gratitude to Me and to thy parents; to Me is thy final goal".

b) Keeping contracts and promises and fulfilling all obligations.

c) Honest and correct accounting of the properties of wards, orphans and widows.

d) Charity and help, which should not be advertised and should never be a matter for reproach.

e) There should be neither niggardliness nor waste.

f) Falsehood, hypocrisy and envy to be completely eschewed.

g) Divorce: For the first time in the history of marital relations, the unrestricted practice and harsh manner of divorce, prevalent before the advent of Islam, were replaced by very humane regulations for making divorced women's lot easy.

h) No testator can withhold or deny the right of heirs.

i) Intoxicants and gambling, two great evils, to be strictly avoided.

j) Hospitality, social properties and personal courtesies to be observed on all occasions. The result has been, the Muslims amongst all people excel in this respect.

k) Acquisition of knowledge at any cost or trouble.

l) Respect for other religions, a fact which the non-Muslims, except the well-informed amongst them, deliberately choose to forget or suppress. Quran's injunction is clear: "There is no compulsion in religion". And in the chapter Al-Kafirun God directs Muhammad to say to the unbelievers — "Unto you your religion and unto me my religion". Do not wrangle with others over matters pertaining to religicus observances.

m) Courtesy, kindness and help to neighbours on all occasions.

n) Do not slander women; and do not talk ill of persons behind them.

o) Do justice between man and man. Fail not in giving correct weight and measure.

p) The following four foods are prohibited.

1. Blood 2. An animal that has died of itself (*i.e.* carrion)

3. Flesh of swine 4. That on which the name of other than God has been pronounced before being killed for purpose of food.

The fourth prohibition includes fruits, food and drink offered to idols and images.

There are many other excellent precepts but those that I have described above give an idea of the Islamic code of conduct and way of life, which lead to full development of individuals and nations, and which fuse faith, worship and day-to-day life into a harmonious whole.